The Fire Station

by Gail Saunders-Smith

Content Consultant:
Timothy Elliott
International Association of Fire Chiefs

Pebble Books
an imprint of Capstone Press

A fire station is where fire fighters work. Fire fighters keep their trucks and supplies at the fire station. Fire fighters and fire trucks must be ready to go at all times.

Dispatchers work with fire fighters. Dispatchers tell fire fighters where fires are. Dispatchers call fire fighters over radios.

Fire fighters must dress quickly. They keep their clothes ready. Heavy pants and jackets protect their bodies. Heavy boots protect their feet from sharp objects. Protect means to keep safe.

Fire fighters wear helmets. Helmets protect their heads from falling objects. Helmets also protect their faces.

Fires make a lot of smoke. Smoke makes it hard for people to breathe. Fire fighters wear air tanks and masks at a fire. The air in the tanks helps fire fighters breathe.

Fire stations have many trucks. Fire trucks carry tools for putting out fires. Some trucks carry hoses. Fire fighters use hoses to spray water on fires.

Fire fighters use tanker trucks to carry water to some fires. Tanker trucks have large tanks. The tanks hold water to put out fires.

Ladder trucks carry ladders. Each truck has one tall ladder on top. This ladder unfolds to reach high places. Some ladders have a basket at the top. Fire fighters stand in this basket.

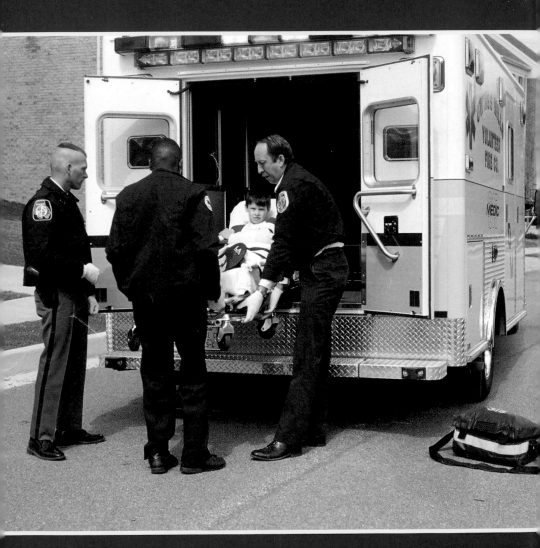

Some trucks carry first aid supplies. Fire fighters give first aid to people who are hurt. All fire fighters work to save people and buildings.

Words to Know

dispatcher—a person who answers calls and sends fire fighters to fires

first aid—medicine and tools used to help people who are hurt or sick

helmet—a hard hat that keeps a person's head safe

hose—a long, bendable tube that carries water from one place to another

ladder—a metal or wood tool that people climb to reach high places

protect—to keep safe

spray—to make water come out of a hose quickly

Read More

Ready, Dee. *Fire Fighters.* Community Helpers. Mankato, Minn.: Bridgestone Books, 1997.

Simon, Norma. *Fire Fighters.* New York: Simon & Schuster Books for Young Readers, 1995.

Smyth, Iain. *Zoom, Zoom Fire Engine!* New York: Crown Publishing, 1997.

Internet Sites

Fire Safe Kids Main Page
  http://www.state.il.us/kids/fire

NFPA Fire Facts and Lore FAQs
  http://www.nfpa.org/fireFactsNLore.html

USFA Kids Homepage
  http://www.usfa.fema.gov/kids/index.htm

Index/Word List

Word Count: 237
Early-Intervention Level: 12

Editorial Credits
Lois Wallentine, editor; James Franklin, design; Michelle L. Norstad, photo research

Photo Credits
Betty Crowell, cover, 14
Dembinsky Photo Associates, Inc./Jim Regan, 18
Emergency!Stock/Howard M. Paul, 6, 16; Jeffry M. Meyers, 8
William B. Folsom, 12
Photo Network /Tom Tracy, 4; Stephen Agricola, 20
Valan Photos/Phillip Norton, 1, 10